A Book of Poems

Expressions From Within

Written By: Barbara J. Boggs

Copyright © 2014 by Barbara J. Boggs

A Book of Poems
Expressions From Within
by Barbara J. Boggs

Printed in the United States of America

ISBN 9781628719369

All rights reserved solely by the author. The author guarantees all contents are original and do not infringe upon the legal rights of any other person or work. No part of this book may be reproduced in any form without the permission of the author. The views expressed in this book are not necessarily those of the publisher.

www.xulonpress.com

Table of Contents

Acknowledgements vii
Introduction ix

Journey To Happiness 11
Fear No Change 13
A Couple Is 14
Promises of Love 15
Search For The Right Man 16
WHY LORD 18
Why Am I With You? 20
Wake Up! 23
I Am Not For Sale 25
Reflections 26
Tomorrow Isn't Promised 27
Procrastination 28
Through His Eyes 29
Dreams 31
Love For A Moment 32
Confident Woman 33
Bad Relationship 34
Unexpectantly 35

Acknowledgements

I would like to thank my husband and children for their support as I was writing this book. I could not have completed this book of poems had I not had their understanding and help with pitching in around the house. I also would like to thank my friends who certainly gave me encouragement to follow my dreams. Lastly, I thank God for opening up my heart. So, that I could hear the cries of my sisters whose hearts have been broken. I thank God for pouring into me his words to be shared with those in need of hope and encouragement and in search of true love.

Introduction

This is a book of inspirational poems written to bring joy, peace, encouragement and hope to its readers. Each poem was written from the heart of the author in response to the cries of the broken hearted, hopeless, lost, confused and hopeless romantic.

Journey To Happiness

I discovered I wasn't alone on this journey,
I had traveling companions along with me.
It was very surprising for me to see,
That they had a great influence on me.
The roads that I chose to travel on my journey,
Wasn't really a choice that was made by me.
My traveling companions were so very strong,
But I had to somehow go on my journey alone.
And if I get lost along the way,
I know I will find the right path one day.
And if there are times when I fall down,
I know I will be able to pick myself up off the ground.

I no longer want these traveling companions to think for me,
With prayer and strength I know I can be free.
I have let them be in control for so very long,
But now I want to handle my life on my own.
In the past I thought I needed their protection,
Afraid to live, enjoy and have fun.
Punishing myself for what had been done to me,
Refusing to let myself believe that I could one day be happy.

Deciding that true love wasn't what I wanted anymore,
Allowing my traveling companions to close the true love door.
Any one bringing extravagant gifts could have me,
Cause who needs love when they got money.
Man, bring me gifts, money and all the fancy things,

This will keep my mind off love and a wedding ring.
Do with me what you want, I don't care,
My heart has already been broken and it's beyond repair.
Given up on all hope for love was where I was right then,
And unable to believe that true love can come around again.

Then one day my eyes were opened wide,
Something was tugging and pulling from inside.
It was as if there was a battle from within,
And that something I felt was determined to win.
Suddenly the gifts and money wasn't appealing to me,
Now, all I wanted was to be set free.
But my traveling companions hold was so strong,
No matter how I tried to shake them they kept hanging on.
They filled me with such intensity from my toes to my head,
I no longer saw black, now I saw red.
Thoughts of all the times I had found love but was mislead,
Suddenly I had a strong urge to bring blood to their heads.
But this warm feeling emanated from the center of my stomach throughout my body,
And amazingly I could feel myself break free.
Look at this smile on my face, was it really me?
Now inside and out I was a projection of beauty.
It was clear to me that the time was finally here,
To say good bye to my traveling companions- anger, hatred, unforgiving, revenge and fear.
Finally I could find the path to true love,
Something that I had been dreaming of.
The path visible by a bright light for to see,
Much to my surprise was illuminating from me.
So my journey to happiness has come to an end,
Cause now I know with man it does not depend.
For I had true love all along in me.

Fear No Change

Sometimes a change is hard.
But it's the best thing for you,
And moving on to bigger and better things is what you need to do.
Forgetting about the old days and welcoming the new ones,
Ready to start a new life that is filled with excitement and fun.

But every time you try to leave the past behind,
Those few and far between good memories flood your mind.
And before you know it your courage to leave is gone.
Fear sets in and glues your feet down,
But don't let fear stop you from exploring new ground.
Cause ahead of you awaits a whole big world for you to see,
And plenty of new people to meet.

So, don't worry about starting the journey alone,
Cause before you know it you'll be singing that "I'm in love again song."

A Couple Is

A couple is strong, united and able to function as one,
With two minds working together committed to getting the job done.
Sometimes in agreement and sometimes not,
But never do they argue about what the other got.
Trusting the other to do the right things,
So they attach their worries to wings and let them fly away.
Always considerate of the others feelings,
And careful with the words they say.
They only want to make the other smile,
And bathe in their laughter for awhile.
They do not cause pain, sadness or despair from the start,
For it would be like stabbing the other in the heart.
They love each other just the same,
Able to feel when the other is in pain.

They are two minds functioning as one,
Loving each other and having lots of fun.
Connected from something deep inside,
Not even thoughts can they hide.
Willing to share and give freely,
For they understand it is not just about me.

Promises of Love

God sent you from above,
For me to cherish and love.
No more standing alone,
Or dining for one at home.
I know God sent you to me to make me whole.
So As I prepare my bed only for you,
I promise to forever remain true.
Together we will make it through,
No matter what challenges lie ahead for me and you.
As long as we continue to pray,
United as one we will stay.
I promise to be strong when you are weak,
And when you are cold I'll be your heat.
No more dark stormy nights,
For you fill my life with embracing warm light.
I promise I will be your bright and shining star,
And be there to guide you no matter where you are.

Search For The Right Man

I have been searching my whole life,
For a man to take me as his wife.
Wanting to find that perfect love you see,
That I believe is worthy of me.
With my standards high I search the land,
Confident that I will find that perfect man.
Unwilling to accept nothing less from anyone,
Cause I know that I'll find the best in the long run.
I know that kind of man that would be good for me,
It sure ain't a broke man nor will it ever be.
I'll wait cause I know true love is coming one day,
So, I ain't trying to let a man I don't want get in the way.
In the meantime though, I'll go out, party and have some fun,
Talk to Mr. Ed and just about anyone.
But when the lights come on and the night comes to an end,
It is not a surprise that not one brother could get the win.
Oh, they fought hard and brought all their best lines to me,
But in the end, it was me that felt like Mohammed Ali.

But time is growing near and my clock is ticking fast,
I may have to reconsider the man from my past.
What am I doing wrong, why can't I get it right?
Don't these guys know I'm the best thing that they will ever have in their life.
I don't want to settle cause I see what my friends got.
They got a man but love they did not.
I want true love you see,
It is everything to me.
For I like the way it feels, all tingly inside.

That's why I'm willing to search for it worldwide.
I know love is kind, everlasting and strong.
But the guys I meet say, "Don't gain weight or I'm gone."

I know love is patient and never asks for anything in return.
But the guys I date say, "What are you going to give me? I ain't waiting till hell burns."
Love is not rude, self-seeking or rough,
But the guys I meet say, "Girl this is mine. You betta get your own stuff."
For this reason I am still alone,
I know what love is and these guys are all wrong.

Without love I am nothing so what must I do?
That's why Lord I am bringing this question to you.
So the Lord said, "Child stand still and listen to me.
The man you want is not who you need.
You've been searching and moving all across the land.
While the man you need was trying to grab your hand.
My child stop moving and look no more.
Let the man you need walk through your door.
I have told the man you need all about you.
So pay attention cause it's not what he says, but it is what he chooses to do.
This man I send for you to see,
May not be driving a fancy car, wearing fine clothes or expensive jewelry.
But don't you doubt that this is the man you need,
Cause he brings love for you unconditionally."

WHY LORD

Why Lord is this happening to me,
Why doesn't he let me be?
I'm a good person I follow the rules,
But he just laughs and calls me a fool.
I was told education would set me free,
Then why are these chains still on me.
I work hard each and every day,
But he says if I rest I will lose my pay.
And what about my children I have at home,
Can't afford to hire help, so I have to leave them alone.
So I pray, "Lord don't let me get ill",
For I can't pay the hospital bill.

Lord, I know you say bring you my worries,
But no time to pray, cause I'm always in a hurry.
And I count, "one, two, three and four",
I watch my money go right out the door.
It all goes even the pennies, nickels and dimes,
It's sad to me that it all belongs to others and none is mine.

I'm sorry Lord, I can't do what you say,
Cause I have nothing left to tithe on Sunday.
Lord, why are all these troubles coming to me?
You say pray and I do, down on one knee.
I don't have time to deal with my brother's baby mama,
So I turn my back, cause I got my own drama.

I'm a good Christian you see,
Cause when I can, I give to the needy.
I am not perfect but I do believe in Christianity,
But that doesn't mean I'm going to let people walk all over me.

Turning the other cheek might have been fine back then,
But times have changed, you hit me and I'm going for your chin.
Lord, don't get me wrong I'm not going to start a fight,
But I will do what it takes to prove I'm right.

Lord I pray to you for help when I can,
You don't answer me, but you answer my friend.
She's always saying, "The Lord told me this and the Lord told me that",
But, when am I going to get an answer back.

Then one day much to my surprise,
I heard the Lord say, "Child open your eyes".
He said, "Trouble was sent to bring you to me,
And when you came, your troubles were gone and you were set free,
Only to go another day without thinking of me.
It was clear, my child, that you didn't hear what I had to say,
Cause you insisted on doing things your way.
I said get down on both knees to pray, but each time you came,
It was on one knee that day.
I gave you money to pay all your bills and more,
But when your brother came in need,
You just closed the door.
And after all of this, on Sunday when you come,
And it is time to show me some love,
But you show me you have none,
So quickly you forget from where your blessings come.
Still my child, I love you unconditionally,
But if you want to be trouble free, then stop take time and listen to me."

Why Am I With You?

I don't need you to validate me,
I finally understand that there is no we.
But for so many years I waited on you,
While you decided what you wanted to do.
So many other opportunities I let pass me by,
Cause I was holding on to a life filled with lies.
But no more! no more!
Did I wear a sign over my heart that said "Take it, it's free?"
I feel like that's what you did to me.
Never did you give to me,
A love that was true and condition free.
I used to think that you were my life,
And all I wanted was to be your wife.
Everyday I worked hard to please you,
Thoughts of something to do that was new.
I often wondered, "Why am I with you?"
It is obvious to me you don't appreciate me or anything that I do.
Each and everyday I give you my all,
I cook, clean and even iron your drawls.
But never do you support me in things that I want to do,
In fact, you threaten me and say, "If you don't do this, then we're through."
And when I'm happy, smiling and feeling all tingly inside,
You find a way to make my happiness die.

I used to let you treat me any way,
Cursing and abusing me on any given day.
Disrespecting me with other women that you said were just your friends,
Only to find out you lied cause it was my bed they were in.
I can't believe I turned away from my friends and family,
Listening to you tell me, "Baby forget them, you've got me."
But, No more! No more!

Why am I with you?
Cause I am not happy,
You do nothing to please me.
It's all about pleasing you and everyone can see,
That it's clear that there is no we.
Ten years and two babies,
And you still have not committed to me.
Can the handwriting on the wall be any clearer to see?

Why am I with you?
Is it just to pay the bills for me,
Or put food on the table for our family.
Cause I can find someone else to do this in time,
And for him having one woman would be just fine.
Someone willing to raise the kids with me,
And I won't have to worry about him chasing every woman he sees.

So, why am I with you?
Am I waiting for you to open your eyes to see,
That you have a real treasure in me?
Am I waiting on you to change your ways?
Cause that's not going to happen, not even in a hundred more days.
Am I still waiting on you to show me the kind of love,
That I am so very much deserving of?
Am I hoping the common bond we share with our baby boy and girl,
Is enough to keep us together so we don't destroy their world?
No more! No more!

Then, why am I with you?
If it is not any of these things,
And this is the best that you can bring.
Life is too short to settle for this kind of stuff,
But this will never end until I feel I've had enough.
Cause this situation is obviously beneficial to you,
But the benefits to me is so clearly few.

So now it is time for me to do what is long overdue,
And no more will I have to ask, "Why am I with you?"

Wake Up!

Black People wake up and open your eyes.
Stop looking at each other with hatred, despair and despise.
Never a kind word to say,
Refusing to show love to each other no matter what the day.

Black People, wake up and open your eyes.
Don't raise your hand against your brother,
Stop planning and conspiring to hurt each other.
Committing violent acts till no end,
Rather than to be another black person's friend.

Black People, wake up and open your eyes.
Swear not to tell your brother another lie.
Say what you mean and mean what you say,
Character and trust is built this way.
Give to each other and expect nothing in return,
For it's okay to be all about concern.
Give a helping hand, you got two,
Wouldn't you want someone to do this for you?

Black People, wake up and open your eyes.
Put an end to this violence before another brother dies.
Cherish, respect and love one another,
Don't give truth to others believes about your color.

And listen to me brother,
Don't you love your mother?
Then how can you raise your hand,
To do harm to your woman.
This is not what God would have you to do,

For he made woman from part of you.
She's yours to love with all your might,
Not curse, disrespect, degrade or fight.

Black People, wake up before it's too late.
Stand strong hand in hand from state to state.
Spread the word to each other to love not hate.
Share words to each other of encouragement and wisdom,
Don't you know that is how our ancestor's gained their freedom?

Walk the path for your children to see,
That this is the way to go, follow me.
No reason to be ashamed of your past,
As long as the lessons learned, a life time last.

Black People, vow to make a change this day.
Chose to look at each other in a more positive way.
Just because you got your water first,
Don't forget about your brother behind you who thirsts.
When you see your brother has fallen down,
Reach out and lift him off the ground.
Be careful not to judge another you see,
What happened to your brother could happen to you or me.

So, Black People go and hold your head up high,
And let your light illuminate the sky.
The next time you see your brother, flash him a smile,
And don't be afraid to stop to chat for awhile.
Let your hearts be filled with love for all to see,
Because it is the power of love that will once again set us free.

I Am Not For Sale

Listen to me I have something to say,
I will not let you treat me this way.
I am a person just like you,
I have a voice and I want to be heard too.
You can buy beans, bread and peas,
But you can not buy me.
For I am a human being in case you can't tell,
And I am not for sale.

Yes I look different from you,
And I don't come from this land this is true.
But we are the same, you and me,
And I deserve to be treated equally.
Cause when you go to the store to buy bread,
Nowhere on the shelf do you see my head.
For I am a human being in case you can't tell,
And I am not for sale.

I can do many things you see,
But I do not work for free.
I will work hard every day,
But I want to receive an equal pay.
I know you know what I can do,
My strength and intelligence is appealing to you.

So don't pretend to confuse me with an animal species,
For they walk on all fours and have a tail,
And I walk on two feet and speak very well.
So, listen closely to me when I say,
I am not for sale!

Reflections

Reflections from a life that has passed,
Memories from a life once had.
Some good and some bad,
But the good ones are few and fade over time,
And the bad ones are embedded deep in my mind.
Distorting my vision and causing my feelings to constantly change,
Filling me with anger and causing me great pain.
Unable to experience those feelings of joy but tired of being mad,
Haunted by those memories from a life once had.
With forgiveness and peace I can find my way,
To feel love and happiness again one day.

Tomorrow Isn't Promised

I do not want this day to leave,
Without fulfilling God's purpose for me.
No matter how many things get in the way,
I can not let it stop me from making the most of today.
No sense looking back at what could have been,
It only wastes time that God has given.
I must not pass up opportunities,
To share the gifts that God has given me.
I can't wait for things to be just right,
Cause tomorrow isn't promised and neither is tonight.

Now is the time for me to say,
I love you more than yesterday.
And I thank God for sending you to me,
Cause you make me so very happy.
I would travel to the other side of the world to be with you,
Cause with you in my life there is nothing I can't do.
Adam loved Eve no matter what she put him through,
That is the same way that I feel about you.
I didn't want this day to come to an end,
Without letting you know you are my best friend.
Tomorrow isn't promised this I know to be true,
That is why I must say each and every day how much
I love you.

Procrastination

No time like the present to get the job done,
Why wait on something that may never come.
But even if tomorrow makes it through,
Things left undone gets combined with the new.
Today is filled with so many things to do,
Cause yesterday's things wasn't attended to.
It's easy to say, "I'll get to it later,"
But later never comes cause time is not in your favor.
Stress, panic and frustration is what today brings,
Cause you didn't handle yesterday's things.

Through His Eyes

I had a dream last night,
That I was a star shining bright.
I shined my light across the land,
And touched the hearts of every man.
Where there was darkness I brought light,
And sadness and pain disappeared with the night.
Compelled to travel near and far,
Whenever someone prayed for a shining star.
Poverty and sickness were no more,
Erased by my light beamed down from the sky I soared.
There was no place that I wouldn't go,
As long as there were people who needed me so.

And when I stopped to rest for a spell,
Suddenly my ears were pierced by unbearable yells.
Then again I soared across the skies,
Pulled in the direction of the excruciating cries.
Uplifting spirits and spreading joy,
And assisting in the birth of a baby boy.
The things I could do was amazing to me,
I could kiss the ground and up would come a tree.
I could blow on the ocean and calm the waters down,
And hold my hand over the land and stop tornadoes from touching the ground.
And in times of turmoil, conflict and war,
I could wave my hand and fighting would be no more.

But I couldn't help but wonder about this dream,
Cause my eyes were wide open or at least it seemed.
And I couldn't explain this light I felt inside of me,
It was warm and burned bright and shined intensely.
Nor did I know why the problems I had yesterday,
Seemed so small and unimportant in every way.
The worries I had were no more,
After my travel across the sky I soared.
I know that things have changed for me,
For before I was blind but now I see.

It was at this time it made sense to me,
I wasn't traveling alone in this dream you see.
The light that illuminated the sky,
Did not come from me but from someone way up high.
And as I traveled across the land,
I was holding someone's hand.
It was through this person's eyes,
That I was able to see as I soared the skies.
And the pain I could feel was not mine alone,
But it came from Him touched by the peoples moans.

Dreams

I often wondered why we dream,
What's the importance and why does it seem,
That it's more than just physical and biological things,
It's something more than what I'm understanding.
All I know is that when I dream,
I go to a place that I've never seen,
It's beautiful, safe and peaceful,
And sometimes there are people there I know.
While I'm there no worries about time or places to be,
Or anything that might be stressful to me.
I can be anything that I want to be,
The sky is the limit cause I am free.
Nothing can make my eyes tear,
No pain can ever reach me here.
When I am awake I can not see,
But in my dreams nothing is blurry.
I don't have to hide that I look differently,
And I am still treated equally.
I can hold my head up high and stand tall for all to see,
Cause I am not afraid of what people might do to me.
In this place I believe anything is possible,
All I have to do is will it and it will be so.
Nothing can hurt me in any way,
I control my life and the events of my day.

Love For A Moment

Love can be instant and last just for a moment.
And in that time it satisfies your hearts desires.
It can be just what you need it to be
To release you from past pain and agony.
One tender stroke across your hand
Can erase sour memories like the wind across foot prints left in the sand.
A long awaited gentle touch,
Comes at a time when it is needed so much.
Lost until this love came along,
To remind you of a feeling once known.

Directing your attention to all the beautiful things,
And forgetting about all the pain that life brings.
Just for a moment you have no worries or cares,
It almost seems as if you are floating on air.
Feeling all good and tingly inside,
Hypnotized by love like a groom to his bride.

Love so deep but only a moment lasts,
How can something so good be gone so fast?
It was never meant to stay for very long,
But to heal your heart and make you strong.
After a moment it is time to let it go,
But your paths will meet again, this you know.

Confident Woman

I know who I am, I am she,
I am a creation of God's artistry.
Made out of love, strength, intelligence and great insight,
Carefully molded until all was just right.
I have a plan to reach my goal,
Distractions and obstacles will not be in control.
Doubt and uncertainty are not a part of my vocabulary,
Cause decisions to make come easy for me.
When ever a problem comes my way,
I can find a solution on any given day.
My thoughts are clear and flow freely.
Like the waters that flow in the Caribbean Sea.
I trust in myself to guide me through the storms of life,
For I know that I have what it takes to over come the strife.
It is clear for me the way to go,
I don't rely on guesses, but on what I know.
I am confident about who I am , I am she,
Because of this, man questions my identity.
But make no mistake, I know my role,
I am a woman who is confident about what she knows.

Bad Relationship

I was lost but now I am found.
No more walking with my head hanging down.
It doesn't matter what you say,
I'm going to love me anyway.
I let the words that you fed me,
Stop me from fulfilling my destiny.
Unable to move unless you told me where to go,
But now I make my own decisions based on what I know.

Weak as a wounded deer,
And paralyzed with so much fear
Of your wrath that would fall on my head,
If I didn't follow as I was led.
Trembling I would fall to my knees,
And pray to God to forever set me free.

I wanted this suffering to be no more,
So I asked God to open wide the door.
And bless me with the strength to pass through,
Able to begin a life brand new.
If God would just give me this opportunity,
I promise to forgive and be thankful for what has been given to me.
No longer will one look at me and see sadness and fear,
Cause now I stand tall and with love I will persevere.

Unexpectantly

Sometimes things happen rather unrepentantly,
And to question why isn't for you or me.
There is something more powerful from up high,
That knows the answer to the question why.
Embrace the unexpectant and make the most of it,
Don't use it for a reason to quit.
Just because it wasn't planned for,
Doesn't mean it has to block any open doors.

Everything can't be planned perfectly,
Cause some things are controlled by powers not from you or me,
To make us strong as iron
Able to defeat the attacks of a lion,
Or to open our eyes so we can see
The path to travel that lead us to victory
Or to reveal secrets so things are more clearly
To release us from the lies that influenced our destiny.
Unexpectantly, Is this really true?
Or, could it be that someone is looking out for me and you?

www.ingramcontent.com/pod-product-compliance
Lightning Source LLC
LaVergne TN
LVHW021744060526
838200LV00052B/3463